Waterways at Work

Anderton in Cheshire. A River Weaver scene from the 1950s. Below the salt chutes the steam powered packet *Weaver Belle*, a narrow boat from the local firm of Seddons, together with the dumb barge *Gowanburn* show the wide variety of craft that once worked upon our waterways. At one stage boats like these helped to transport over a million tons of salt down the river each year.

Waterways at Work

Thomas Pellow

With illustrations by
Edward Paget-Tomlinson

The Landscape Press

First published in Great Britain in 2000 by

The Landscape Press
Kimbolton, Herefordshire

ISBN 0 947849 74 2

Printed by Johnsons of Nantwich Limited

CONTENTS

INTRODUCTION

It is perhaps too easy to take our current transport systems for granted and instead bemoan their various shortcomings. Our commercial existence is grounded in the need to be able to move raw materials and manufactured goods, people and information speedily, reliably and economically across our own country and beyond. Yet little over two hundred years ago the situation was very different, economic development being hampered and constrained by the lack of adequate inland transport. The history of the industrial revolution and the emergence of our modern industrialised society is closely bound up with the development of a parallel transport system able to move goods and people efficiently - and in this the waterways were to prove the crucial element in the early years; albeit eventually overtaken and to a large extent replaced by railways, and later still by modern road networks.

This book does not set out to present a detailed chronological history of these developments - for such works already exist. Neither does it set out to describe how physical improvements were made to rivers to make them more navigable, nor how the canals that followed were planned and built. These topics are covered in the companion work to this volume - *Waterways in the Making.*

Instead it sets out to show something of what working life was like on the waterways, in their heyday and more recently : what they carried, how goods were handled, how the boats were built and worked - and something of the isolated and often harsh existence of the boat people who made all of it possible.

For most of us our encounters with waterways are with the narrow canals of the midlands, for these form the core of what have become the recreational cruising grounds of today. These canals were central to what can now be seen as a transport revolution - and as such receive appropriate emphasis. But the significant role of river navigations and broad canals is not ignored. Our larger rivers and their estuaries were carrying goods to and from inland destinations before the days of widespread industrialisation, and many continue to do so today. However it is the quintessentially English phenomenon of working narrow boats that provides the main focus here, for it is on the narrow canals that the boater of today is mainly to be found - and on these same waters that many of the early stages of industrialisation were to depend.

CARGOES AND CARRYING

When in 1775 the Horsehay Iron Company - from its foundry near present day Telford in Shropshire - wished to transport manufactured goods to Chester it had a choice. It could either send them forty miles overland, or instead by water. This latter journey involved a passage down the River Severn, transhipment to a coastal craft and a sail powered journey out into the Bristol Channel, around the length of the Welsh coast and eventually into the estuary of the River Dee and on to Chester. The waterborne alternative, a journey of nearly four hundred miles, was chosen as the more effective route.

Prior to the transport revolution, that went hand in hand with the industrialisation of the late18th century, the roads of England and Wales had seen virtually no improvements since the departure of the Romans. In most cases they showed such signs of neglect as to make them virtually impassable in the winter. Being the responsibility of the parishes through which they passed there was no national overview of transport needs, nor much local concern for through traffic. Thus such indefegatible travellers as Arthur Young, who wrote extensively of his travels in the 18th century, referred to "execrable and barbarous roads" - while others even went to Court in attempts to force the parishes to do something about their roads.

But if the passage for horsemen and walkers was difficult enough, matters were even worse when it came to the carriage of goods. Strings of pack horses, each animal only able to carry about an eighth of a ton (125 kgs), attempted to cater for the needs of commerce - but bad weather and winter could make already slow and unreliable progress even harder if not impossible. Much trade, and associated economic activity, was obliged to remain local and seasonal as only limited transport of bulky goods for any distance was readily possible - except by water. As a result proximity of the coast, an estuary or a navigable river was immensely advantageous to the location of an industry; boats had long proved to be the most effective way of moving bulky, heavy and fragile goods.

Much of the land mass of England and Wales is within a score of miles of the sea and the tidal reaches of rivers. So it was that a variety of little ships evolved; built to suit local conditions and able to undertake a wide range of carrying duties. These worked from small wharves, quays and even beaches - and combined with horse and cart served the hinterlands behind the coast. In such areas, where the coastline was made up of a mass of little creeks and inlets, the shortest distance between two points was often by water and small sailing barges proved an essential part of local transport provision. Such was the case in the south west peninsula, along some parts of the south coast, up the Thames estuary and into the rivers and Broads of East Anglia. Further north other specialised sailing craft worked up the River Humber, the River Trent and the Yorkshire Ouse; while on the west coast the local design of sailing "flats" traded on the muddy waters of the Mersey estuary.

The scene pictured *opposite* shows the barge "Shamrock" unloading at Cothele on the River Tamar that separates Cornwall from Devon; a typical scene from around the year 1900. Usually worked as an "inside" boat she traded locally from estuary to estuary and up tidal rivers, rather than making more exposed sea passages as did larger "outside" boats. Her masts are mounted in tabernacles to allow them to be lowered when passing under river bridges-so extending her working range. Such west country barges were usually from 40 to 50 feet long (12 to 15 metres) and with a small cabin to accommodate a crew of two. About 50 tons could have been carried. Bulk cargoes, such as the timber seen here on the quay side, together with the rocks and minerals from this rich quarrying and mining area made up many of her pay loads. Boats that specialised in this type of work were often known as "stone boats" with limestone and coal for burning at waterside kilns being an important cargo.

"Shamrock" - now jointly preserved by the National Maritime Museum and the National Trust - is shown unloading a cargo of general goods into the wagon that will then be hauled up to destinations in the steep wooded valleys that abound in this area of Cornwall. Despite the coming of the railway in the mid 18th century the difficulties of such local terrain allowed the horse and wagon to remain competitive as local inland carriers well into the 20th century.

Our longest river, the Severn, penetrates far inland. The Romans had used it for the transport of goods, and since the Middle Ages it has been protected by statute as a river to be kept free for navigation, boats once trading from Bristol up past Shrewsbury to Pool Quay near Welshpool, a journey of some 160 miles. By about 1750 there were over three hundred boats trading on the river and with the industrial revolution well underway, and the growing importance of the Ironbridge region, this number was to rise to nearly a thousand. The late 19th century scene pictured *right* shows something of the river at its peak with two of the flat bottomed Severn trows so characteristic of its waters. Each river and estuary had such distinct features as to cause local designs to emerge, best suited to the particular circumstances of the waters concerned. The trows used on the lower Severn were built with distinctive D shaped transoms, their flat bottoms making them much easier to move when they went aground on the many shallows and mudbanks of the navigation. Although they carried a single square rigged mainsail working up stream almost always involved muscle power - at first provided by gangs of bow hauliers, and later on by horses with the completion of a towing path to Shrewsbury in 1812 . The larger boats that worked further down stream, and out into the Bristol Channel often carried fore and aft rig to allow them to cope with the open waters of the seaway, and were also decked. Those that worked on the upper reaches had open holds. As with so many of the waterways associated with industrial sites, manufactured goods and quarried materials were brought down to the water's edge on a horse drawn tramroad. Here a wooden crane is being used to load a trow from the tramroad's wagons. The elegant Ludcroft warehouse, seen in the background, is now part of the Ironbridge Gorge Museum.The Severn has seen an immense amount of trade and for many years was one of the busiest rivers in Europe. Coal and manufactured iron goods from the Ironbridge area went down stream, together with lead, timber and agricultural goods from Shropshire and salt from Droitwich. A variety of imported goods, inclusive of wines and spirits from Bristol, travelled upstream and beyond.

Along with most other river navigations the Severn suffered from a number of major drawbacks. In the summer periods of drought would considerably restrict the depth of available water, making shallower sections difficult if not impossible to pass. In the winter high rainfall and flooding caused such strength of current as to make upstream navigation virtually impossible and downstream work highly dangerous. If improvements could be made to deepen, straighten and calm these rivers, then their navigation could be considerably enhanced.

During the whole of the 17th century and the early years of the 18th century much work on improving rivers was carried out. Particularly notable were the trend setting improvements made to the River Wey as completed in 1653. Of the fifteen mile journey from the Thames up to Guildford nearly half the distance comprised sections of artificially dug waterway. Corners were cut and the more difficult stretches of the river by-passed. Locks and weirs allowed boats to be lifted and lowered, rather than leaving them to the whims of unrestricted current. Further north the rivers Aire and Calder were likewise improved to allow boats passage from the Humber far inland. South again, similar work was to be carried out on the River Kennet to extend navigation from Reading to Newbury; and as was often the case, such developments were angrily opposed by mill owners and other vested interests. Progress however was underway. Thanks to improvements the length of navigable rivers was nearly doubled from seven hundred miles in 1600 to thirteen hundred miles by 1750.

Following close on such river improvements came the beginnings of the canal age proper. In 1755 an Act was obtained to allow "making navigable..... the Sankey Brook". This small and insignificant river provided a potential if restricted route for moving coal from the mines of St Helens in Lancashire down to the River Mersey. Ostensibly the Act was intended to provide for river improvement, but included powers to " make...new cuts". In the event these cuts were so extensive that a canal rather than an improved river emerged - using the Sankey Brook merely for its water supply. While the Act had been exploited to its limit, a point had been made. The booming coalfield and the steady and significant profits of the new Sankey Brook Navigation were a clear indication of the economic potential of specially constructed waterways.

But of all such 18th century work clearly the most significant in changing attitudes and stimulating investment was that of the Bridgewater Canal. From underground waterways that went right up to the coal faces in the Duke of Bridgewater's mines at Worsley, across an extensive embankment and spectacular aqueduct above the River Irwell, it was navigable through to Manchester by 1763. The canal used emerging technology in a bold and imaginative manner and allowed the price of coal supplied to the growing city to be slashed.The profitable transport of bulky goods - so badly needed by the accelerating industrialisation and urbanisation of the times, had been demonstrated. Investors were not slow to respond.

Existing river navigations and early canals were rapidly joined by new and ambitious cuts. A canal to join the Trent and Mersey rivers via the Potteries was authorised in 1766. At the same time the Staffordshire and Worcestershire canal, that was to pass near Wolverhampton and connect with the River Severn, also got its Act. Further south progress on the long planned connection between the Thames and the Bristol Channel was being made as piecemeal development of the Kennet and Avon canal went ahead. The outline of a national waterways network was starting to emerge.

The last few years of the 18th century - and particularly those of 1792 and1793 - are often labelled as those of the Canal Mania. Canals had proved to be by far the most effective way of moving bulk goods - and associated profits seemed there for the taking. Comparisons made by Smeaton and other engineers had shown that a single horse could haul 30 tons along a river and even more on the still waters of a canal. In contrast the loads a pack horse could manage were tiny, while even on the new turnpike roads a horse could only haul a wagon load of about 2 tons. Construction thus began on scores of waterway ventures, some to prove sustainable, but many others wildly over optimistic. The mileage of navigable rivers and canals rose rapidly to well over 3000 miles.

Canals are best suited to the carriage of bulk commodities. Coal and bricks, metallic ores and limestone, fertilisers and timber; these were among the staples of the early waterborne traffic, and remain so today. But although most routes were built with the needs of local mines, quarries and industry in mind, in their early years the waterways also proved effective in the transport of people. By 1767 passenger traffic had started on the Bridgewater canal and was so competitive as to be able to undercut stage coach fares. The majority of canals were to offer provision for passengers in their early years; at first in competition with the stagecoaches on the turnpikes until they both were overtaken by competition from the even newer railways. Particularly successful were the packet boat services on the Lancaster canal pictured *opposite*. With strictly imposed rights of way over other boats the packet boats were hauled along by pairs of horses under the direction of a smartly uniformed and mounted postillion, the helmsman blowing a horn at bridge holes to warn other boats of the rapid approach.

Such journeys offered a high degree of comfort for the time and at first this helped maintain their appeal against their competitors.The bone shaking ride of the roads was replaced by a smooth speedy passage in a carpeted saloon. Tea, coffee and other refreshments were served *en route* and some boats were even heated in winter. In the 1820s the 57 miles between Preston to Kendal were being covered at an average speed of just over four miles per hour. Journey times were steadily reduced, so that by 1839 average speeds had risen to nearly eight miles per hour. On the lock free section between Preston and Lancaster it was taken even higher by the "swift boats" introduced in 1833. Thanks to changes of horses at four mile intervals speeds were pushed up to ten miles per hour on this 30 mile section. For a number of years the packet boat timetables were arranged to fit in with other forms of transport. Connections to the trains at Preston and onward journeys to Manchester and Liverpool were made easy by a service of horse drawn omnibuses, while scheduled stage coaches connected with Chorley and Bolton. But it was not to last. In1840 the parallel railway route illustrated overleaf was opened north of Preston. In the face of this competition packet boat traffic ceased by1846. Here the railways had won.

But more than canal passenger traffic was at risk. Following the initial success of the Liverpool and Manchester Railway - and the doubling of its share price within two years - a new speculative boom was to sweep the country, reaching its peak in the railway mania years of the mid 1840s. In the single year of 1846, over 4500 miles of line were authorised and by 1850 the basic rail network of 6000 miles was virtually complete. To obtain the necessary Acts of Parliament, and in doing so quell the objections of competing canal interests, the railways set out to purchase or lease strategically placed rival waterways. Between 1845 and 1847 nearly 1000 miles of canal were to fall under railway control, and by 1865 a third of the total waterways network had been taken into the hands of these new and largely unsympathetic masters. Legally obliged to keep them open they could however allow them to run down.

Thus ownership of the Kennet and Avon canal fell into the hands of the Great Western Railway in 1852. Unwilling to promote its canal acquisition at the expense of its main railway business it was inevitable that canal traffic should decline and profits fall away. Although some through traffic was to use the canal for another fifty years the route became essentially local in character. The scene pictured *opposite* shows Devizes town wharf in the late 1880s. The flavour is of a quiet, essentially agricultural scene rather than of a busy connection across England joining the Rivers Thames and Avon as originally envisaged.

Across the country many such wharves survived into the early years of the 20th century, their cargoes reflecting the needs of the market towns, villages and rural hinterlands that they served. Grain, limestone, animal feeds and agricultural produce, timber, bricks and coal would be lifted between boat and wharf by muscle power and the aid of a hand operated crane. Horses moved both boats and wagons - but as we are reminded by the gently steaming traction engine in the background of the 1880s scene pictured *overleaf* it was this mechanised form of power that had enabled the railways to so rapidly eclipse the canal.

However not all waterways were to sink into oblivion, for many continued to trade, albeit at varying levels of profitability, alongside their railway rivals for years - some doing so even today. A few railway companies maintained their canal acquisitions as useful adjuncts to their main interests. In 1847 the Trent and Mersey Canal merged with the North Staffordshire Railway which saw how the waterway could serve as a feeder to its Potteries territory. Shipped in via the tidal River Mersey and then unloaded onto narrow boats, a range of clays, flints, felspar, limestone and other bulky potters' materials were carried to the "five towns" - while crated pottery and Cheshire salt went back along the route. Over a million tons of traffic per year was transported on the northern sections of the canal up to the time of the First World War - to continue at reduced levels into the 1960s. The location of so many of the pottery wharves alongside the canal - evisaged by Josiah Wedgwood at the time of the canal's initial promotion - certainly played a large part in maintaining viability for so long.

The illustration on the *opposite* page shows the scene at Weston Point docks at Runcorn in the 1920s. Built by the trustees of the Weaver Navigation - this successful river navigation linked the estuary of the Mersey with the canal running through the main Cheshire salt field and onto the Potteries. At Northwich, where ICI were to establish their chemical works, the Anderton lift allowed boats to be carried between the river and canal above. Narrow boats from the Mersey Weaver and Ship Canal Carrying Company of Stoke, are pictured moored alongside the wharf. A steam crane is shifting potters' materials that have come in by coaster: clay from Cornwall and Dorset, flint from Sussex beaches and Normandy. As will be seen it was a time of great maritime variety, some ships steam driven but many reliant on sail.

From being a largely self sufficient economy at the middle of the 18th century the country steadily developed into a trading nation. The rivers and canals that linked the manufacturing areas with ports and the sea were crucial in getting this process underway and working populations established themselves accordingly.

Weston Point, with its boatmans' church visible in the background, is representative of a number of canal settlements that developed as a direct result of inland navigation.

Sea going craft transhipped loads to the inland waterways at Ellesmere Port at the head of the Shropshire Union, at Goole on the Aire and Calder as well as at Weston Point.

Locks, docks, warehouses and associated boating communities grew up at these places creating, what were in effect, canal towns. On the Severn ships could come far inland to Gloucester Docks - while further upstream a small town was to grow up at Stourport, to mark the point where the Staffordshire and Worcester Canal made its junction with the river.

Canal and river improvements were promoted with profit in mind - income derived from the tolls charged for the use of the waterways. Unlike the railways, that from the outset had been allowed to run their own trains on their own lines, the Acts of Parliament that permitted the building of canals specified that their income was to be derived solely from tolls - and maxima were set for these. Thus independent carriers emerged who operated the boats, paid the tolls and charged their customers an inclusive fee for the carrying service that they provided. Only in the mid 1840s, in an attempt to make canals more competitive with the railways, were the original canal Acts amended to allow the owning companies to operate as carriers as well. While some large canal company owned fleets did emerge - notably on the Shropshire Union routes and the Grand Junction canal - most of the carrying remained in the hands of independents, right up to the time of nationalisation following the Second World War. Tolls were charged to users on a ton per mile basis, and usually took into account the nature of the load; bulky goods, such as coal or stones being charged less per ton than more valuable general merchandise.

Canal owners therefore needed a way by which to establish the loadings of the boats that used their routes. First the boats were "indexed". When empty their freeboard was measured at a number of points. Having established the number of "dry inches" between the gunwales and waterline of the unladen boat, weights were then added, usually in fractions of a ton.

Records were made of the decreasing number of "dry inches" remaining as as the known load went up. These measurements were then published in printed tables and issued to the toll keepers located at junctions and other points along the canal.

When a boat arrived at one of these locations a gauging staff *illustrated left* was placed against the gunwales so that the graduated float within its hollow vertical tube moved up or down to allow a reading of the "dry inches" to be taken. From the pre-prepared gauging tables the boat's load could be read off and the appropriate toll charged. It was not unknown for carriers to attempt to cheat toll collectors. Perhaps an expensive load of general merchandise might be hidden beneath a load of limestone, so that the whole would then be charged at the cheaper rate. As well as being at risk from fraud the toll keepers in the cash based society of early 19th century England were also at risk from theft. In isolated areas it was sometimes necessary for the canal company to arm their employees, so as to protect their takings.

By the 1950s life was less violent, but, as pictured *below* in this scene on the Birmingham Canal Navigations little else seems to have changed. Horse drawn boats are still trading and a gauging stick (staff) is still being used to calculate their loads. The octagonal toll keeper's office is situated on an island site in order to facilitate the measurement and passage of passing boats.

Following their confident and heady early years - and the subsequent shock of having to face up to overpoweringly powerful competition from the railways - the waterways settled down to the realities of the 19th century. Across the country over optimistic and undercapitalised schemes in areas far from suited to canal building were quick to fold. Such a failure was the Leominster Canal, promoted to link Herefordshire with the booming river route of the Severn. Needing immense and expensive engineering works to climb up from the river to the agricultural areas beyond, only its higher middle section was ever built. Although it was to carry local traffic for some fifty years this was never sufficient to generate a dividend for the investors, who were only to get back a fraction of their original outlay when the route was eventually taken over by a railway and suffered the ignominy of being drained.

Other canals were built in more promising locations. Although short of investment for improvement and development once the railways had arrived, they nevertheless managed to trade satisfactorily well into the 20th century. Froghall wharf on the Caldon branch of the Trent and Mersey canal is pictured *above* in a 1920s scene and provides an example. A copper works, a large limestone quarry and associated coal traffic all generated good trade for the route. Here a boat belonging to James Hollinshead, an independent trader from nearby Cheshire, is being loaded with bricks that have been fired in the circular kilns seen behind.

Even at this late date, well over a century after the canal had been opened, the technology has changed little from when it was built. Muscle power dominates as the horse drawn boat is hand loaded from barrows.

In contrast on a number of routes, particularly on northern river derived navigations that are able to carry much larger boats, trading has been continued up to the present time. The illustration *below* shows the staithe that served Denaby Main Colliery on the River Don Navigation in Yorkshire as it appeared in the 1930s. Over twice as wide as a narrow boat ($15\frac{1}{2}$ feet - 4.7metres) these Yorkshire Keels could carry over 100 tons. In this case coal is being loaded from private owner railway wagons for passage down to the docks at Hull. Here it will be taken on board the steam driven trawlers of the fishing fleets that worked from the port until the 1970s. Another notable Yorkshire navigation that continued to flourish is the Aire and Calder, which likewise has had the benefit of ongoing investment to keep it updated and competitive. The River Weaver in Cheshire, pictured in the *frontispiece*, also enjoyed much beneficial improvement during the late 19th century. It was the undercapitalised waterways that had been built in inappropriate areas or on unneeded routes that proved particularly vulnerable to the might of the railways.

The early canals had been built at a time when the outlook of their promoters was strictly local. A national perspective on transport needs had yet to emerge. The task was simply seen as providing a profitable carrying service for the immediate area. A narrowly partisan attitude accordingly informed the early decisions taken by canal companies, adjacent waterways seen as rivals to be either obstructed or ignored. Despite these short sighted local rivalries something of a national picture emerged from attempts made to link the major rivers of the Thames, Trent, Mersey and Severn by a "grand cross" of routes centered on the Midlands. Although this was achieved when the very twisty Oxford canal opened in 1790 a more direct route between the Midlands network and the London was clearly needed. This was to be provided by the completion of the Grand Junction Canal from Paddington to Braunston in 1805. From the outset this was a forward looking company and its strategically important route, although almost entirely used by narrow boats, had been built to wide boat dimensions. Successful in holding off railway competition it did so by reducing tolls, running a short lived carrying operation and making steady improvements. Eventually it was to provide the basis for the new Grand Union Canal Company of 1929 that, by a number of amalgamations, brought the main London, Birmingham and Leicester routes under one single management. Similar amalgamations of carrying fleets also allowed it to establish its own Grand Union Canal Carrying Company in 1934.

Large volumes of trade passed through its Regents Canal Dock, at Limehouse on the Thames as pictured *opposite*. A regular service of steamers from Norway, Germany, Holland and Spain came in through the ship lock and cargoes of every description were discharged overside into waiting Grand Union boats. Timber from Scandinavia, coal for delivery to London power stations and steel for Birmingham were major bulk cargoes. Manufactured foodstuffs, industrial goods and a range of merchandise from the Midlands went back out.

Narrow boats were very much general carriers. While bulky materials such as coal or building materials could be carried in an open hold without protection more perishable and valuable goods needed a watertight and secure covering. In this 1930s scene three narrow boats are "clothing up" for the purpose. The central boat is having its tarpaulin side cloths fitted to provide a shallow protective skirt around the top of the gunwales. They were held in place by "strings" (thin ropes) that are being taken up over the top running planks to the side cloths on the other side, through the eyelets in these - and back over the top plank again before tying down. Top cloths were then unrolled to overlap the side cloths as seen on the left. These were tied to rings on the gunwales with top strings going over. A protective "tippet" - as seen on the right - could be unrolled and secured above before the strings were tied. This reduced any wear from rubbing. At last the cargo was snug and watertight beneath its cloths.

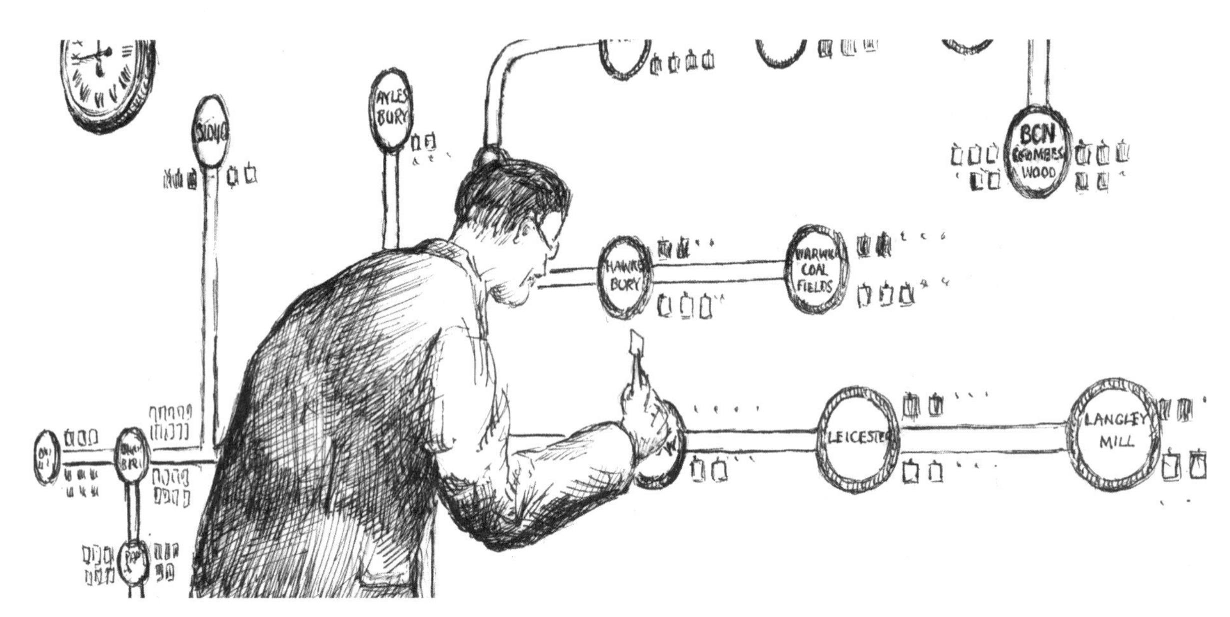

From 1929 onwards the Grand Union was to make determined and imaginative efforts to create a modern waterways network and carrying service able to compete with the railways. Ambitious plans and large investments were made, aided by goverment grant in the depressed financial climate of the 1930s. Efforts were concentrated on the London to Birmingham route with much deepening and lock widening taking place, while what was to prove an over optimistic programme of boat building also got underway. Six miles up from the Thames a large supply and repair depot was established at Bulls Bridge. It was here that the huge wall chart pictured *above* was set up showing the whole of the route mileage and 23 Reporting Office locations along the way. With 380 miles of waterway and 186 pairs of narrow boats available it was evident that some system of information and control was needed if resources could be deployed to best advantage. Each morning information would be passed to Bulls Bridge by note or telephone and the chart updated. Red tags represented the loaded boats and green ones unladen craft. These would be moved to their last reported position and orders, based on a clear picture of the fleet's deployment, could then be given. It was a brave attempt to update the canals in an era dominated by rail and ever increasing road transport. But although canal traffic was substantially increased the financial results were far from good. Post war nationalisation of transport was to provide the way out.

From the other side of Birmingham ran another strategic route. What was to become the main line of the Shropshire Union system was also the last major narrow canal to be built. As the Birmingham and Liverpool Junction it had opened as late as 1835 to join the older Chester Canal at Nantwich and continue the journey northwest to the tidal waters of the Mersey estuary at Ellesmere Port. Pictured *below* is perhaps the most elegant feature ever to have graced a canal town; the magnificent Telford designed warehouse. Graceful flat arches spread out from the wings of the warehouse across the waters of the canal basin so that boats could tie up underneath. Here two Mersey flats, part of the extensive Shropshire Union fleet, that at its peak included over 400 narrow boats and 100 flats, are being unloaded by the hydraulic hoists installed in the 1870s. An immense variety and huge quantity of traffic passed through here. In 1846 the whole of the Shropshire Union system was leased to the London and North Western Railway as were the extensive Birmingham Canal Navigations. Rather than run them down, the railway used these networks well, partly for local trade, partly to block its railway rival, the Great Western, but also to tap the huge overseas trade generated by the Midlands and which could be carried to and from the Mersey and beyond.

To the west the Shropshire Union remained deeply rural; horse drawn boats tying up in locks to unload cargoes of fertiliser and coal in exchange for local produce, timber and stone.

Much of the handling of goods and cargoes, particularly on the narrow canals, remained a matter of muscle and wheelbarrow, right to the end. The waterways were largely an isolated world and most of their technology reflected a 19th rather than 20th century approach - partly through lack of investment but underpinned by deeply ingrained force of habit. Pictured *left* is a 1950s Potteries scene - essentially unchanged from a hundred years before. A pair of local boats from the Anderton Company has come down the Trent and Mersey with a load of felspar. Shovels and barrows are being used to transfer the materials from open holds to the canal side pottery works. Crated potteries products will then be boated away.

The proximity of canal to pottery was one of the factors that allowed the Anderton Company to trade in so anachronistic a way for so long, but many power stations were to make good use of their waterside locations in a more modern manner - and indeed had been built on such sites with coal delivery in mind. Pictured *right* is a scene at the Wolverhampton power station as it also would have appeared in the 1950s. The grab unloads the 'hampton (Wolverhampton) boats that, longer and wider than typical narrow boats, were confined to the lock free route down from the Cannock coalfields.

Liquid cargoes require more specialist handling. The casks and drums of the early years were eventually replaced by specialist craft built with holds turned into tanks. A small number of carrying firms, able to handle oil, petroleum, creosote, tar and the like, established themselves in industrial locations, prominent among them Thomas Clayton's of Oldbury. Their floating tankers were to work down the Shropshire Union from Stanlow oil refinery, Ellesmere Port to the Shell depot at Langley Green in Birmingham until 1955. Pictured *right* one of their tar boats is being pumped out. To drain the last of the liquid into the bows a concrete weight, slung from above, is being used to push the boat down.

While the 1950s saw a rapid decline in trade on the narrow canals it was the harsh winter of 1963, leaving boats trapped in ice for three months, that dealt the terminal blow. A few independent carriers, such as Willow Wren, which took over a number of boats from the disbanded British Waterways fleet, struggled on until 1970 before giving up the impossible struggle to make narrow boat carrying pay. And so today it is on such river navigations as the Severn, Trent, Humber and Thames that limited commercial carrying is mainly found, while on many of the wide canal routes and all of the narrow canals it has been replaced by recreational traffic.

BUILDING THE BOATS

Working boats came in all sorts of shapes and sizes. Among the smallest were the simple wooden tubs that carried coal along the now lost industrial canals of east Shropshire. Virtually floating wooden boxes these could hold about five tons. Linked together by chains as many as twenty such tubs were pulled along in a train behind a single hard working horse. The horse driver, long steering shaft in hand, prodded and poked from the tow path to keep the boats away from the bank. The notion of a train of compartment boats was later taken up and refined on the Aire and Calder and South Yorkshire Navigations where up to thirty large compartment boats could be hauled along behind a tug. The north of England has also been home to some of the largest craft to have worked on our inland waterways. John Harker Ltd, of Knottingley in Yorkshire, has built and worked a series of motorised tanker barges over many years, operating vessels as long as 200 ft (60.9 metres) and 20ft beam (6.1 metres) and capable of shipping 600 tons of oil.

And in between has come the elegance of the inspection launches from which directors and management considered their waterways, the plain utilitarianism of the small canoe - like mine boats that worked into the Duke of Bridgewater's Worsley collieries, and the simple grace of single sailed wherries working up rivers and onto the Norfolk Broads. Something of the wide variety of canal and river craft that have worked in England and Wales is illustrated on *page 79*.

Irrespective of their size or location all the early boats were built of wood. Among the many innovations to spring from the Ironbridge area of Shropshire was the first iron boat. "The Trial" was built and then launched onto the Severn by John Wilkinson in 1787. But it was to take over a hundred years more before iron and steel hulls were seen in any quantity on the waterways. After the great creative and entrepreneurial surge of the late 18th and early 19th centuries waterway confidence and momentum were largely lost. Traditional "low tech" solutions were seen to provide the most cost effective way forward in the context of low investment consequent upon the overshadowing might of the railways.

Wooden boats have a number of practical advantages which helped them maintain their dominance on canals long after most sea going vessels were being built of iron and steel. Small yards with a handful of craftsmen and simple low cost tools were able to build and repair wooden boats without the need for extensive premises or costly steel fabrication equipment. Cheapness and simplicity proved themselves well suited to the essentially basic needs of the waterways. From the 1890s composite boats, with iron sides and wooden bottoms started to be built in significant numbers - while all metal construction was mainly used for such specialist craft as tugs, icebreakers, dredgers and spoil boats - whose hard lives required levels of damage resistance beyond that which wood could easily provide.

The vigorous boat building programme carried out by the Grand Union Canal Carrying Company in the 1930s included the construction of a number of steel built craft - but even in its late attempt to create a modern carrying fleet the Company still commissioned wooden and composite boats. Even after the second World War, when British Waterways did build steel boats, wooden ones continued to be made. "Raymond", the last wooden narrow boat was launched from the old Nurser's boat building yard at Braunston as late as 1958. Nursers was but one of nearly a hundred canalside boatbuilding and repair yards that, between them, supported commercial boating across the Midlands well into the 20th century.

One of the last to continue to operate along totally traditional lines was Ken Keay's dock at Walsall *pictured opposite*. The scene was to change very little from its opening until closure in the 1970's. Such yards ran parallel to the water. Here a narrow boat is being replanked; the boat having been dragged sideways out of the canal then up a slope of planks, using the low geared hand operated winch seen just behind its stem. The new plank being eased into position is cut with a sloping scarf joint at its end. In preference to having vertical joints between the planks, scarf joints were staggered along the strakes (rows of planks) to avoid a line of weakness emerging at any one point. The plank has to carry a curve - so to provide the flexibility needed to get it into shape it has first been steamed in the chest just behind the windlass. From the boiler - in this case an old domestic copper - steam at low pressure is taken into the plank filled chest beyond. Each plank will need about an hour of steaming to make it pliable enough for use. Telephone wires lead down from a telegraph pole to the hut that serves as an office for the yard, while to its right lies the cabin end of an old narrow boat - the "snap hovel" in which the boat builders took their breaks and brewed their tea.

The large open shed, *shown overleaf*, provided a movable area of covered work space. Mounted on wheels it could be pushed up or down to cover the part of the boat to be worked on. The frontage of a yard had to be of a minimum of 70 ft (21 metres) to allow a boat to be hauled up or launched sideways off the bank. Most yards were wide enough to allow more than one boat to be handled at a time while an area of ground space would be taken up by a store of seasoning timber. The stem and stern timbers as well as the side planks were made from oak - while elm, with its natural resistance to rotting while immersed in water, was used for the bottoms. A few boats in the Birmingham area were built of pitch pine, but oak - elm construction was normally used.

To turn these timbers into a working boat was a matter of skill, experience and the use of a simple range of tools as *illustrated opposite*. From Roman days onwards the adze has been the quintessential boat building tool and one is pictured centrally. Similar to an axe its cutting blade is set at right angles to the curved handle. Its use involved swinging it down and often towards oneself - with corresponding risks. The tale is told of a carpenter at the Ellesmere depot on the Shropshire Union who slipped and gashed his leg with an accidental adze blow. He went to where some tar was being softened over a brazier, painted a coating of the hot liquid across the wound to seal it, and went calmly back to his task!

Working clockwise around the picture, bottle shaped "rove bunters" are shown on the ground as used when fixing spikes. Beside these stands a mattock for chopping out rotten wood. The block with holes is a "swage block"- with templates for standard items. Against the anvil are tools of the blacksmiths trade. Most large yards would employ a blacksmith but smaller ones sub - contracted such work. Clamps of various sizes were needed to hold pieces together after steaming and prior to fixing - while a variety of drills and augers,some large enough to drill holes for propeller tubes, are also shown. Saws, chisels and planes complete the top row of the picture while below right is the equipment needed for caulking. This involved forcing oakum (made from old unpicked rope moistened with linseed) into the gaps between planks to make watertight joints. Strands of rolled oakum would be taken from from the three legged caulking bench and hammered into place using the blunt caulking irons shown on the ground. Here, to the left, a "game block" (a spare rudder head) is being used as a makeshift vice - holding a plank firm and ready for cutting.

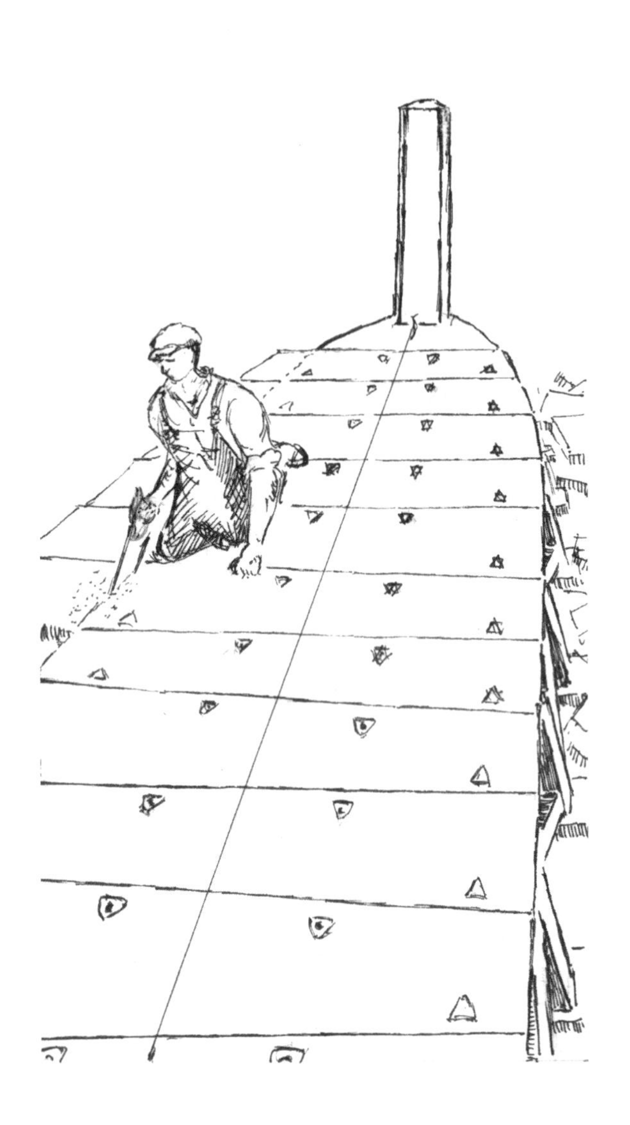

On a platform about $2^{1}/_{2}$ feet (.75 metres) above the ground the bottom planks would be laid out as shown *left*. The centre line, from stem post to stern, shows the eventual position of the keelson. Elm planks were laid at right angles to this, held together by "rampers" - spikes set into concave holes drilled into the planks. "Sawing out," as pictured here, established the plan of the boat. Wooden, or more often metal, "knees" were fixed to the bottom; their gently curved uprights providing the frame to which the side planks were attached. Steamed, clamped and fixed with hammered rivets these side planks were then sealed with "chalico", a flexible waterproofing mix of Stockholm tar, cow dung and horse hair, before being planked in so as to complete the sandwich construction. The keelson, made up of several pieces of scarf jointed timber, was bolted into place and a removable bottom floor placed on either side. The cabin was built onto an oak frame, clad with deal boarding. The boat was now ready for caulking. Once this was completed the hull was painted with red lead inside and blackened outside with pitch, but the bottom elm planks were left unpainted. The time for launching had arrived.

Narrow boats were usually launched sideways - as were most other craft on inland waterways.

There was no room to do otherwise. Large wooden beams were placed under the boat running down the slope from the yard into the water. Onto these would go the heavily greased metal skids on which it was to slide. The boat was jacked up and the frame on which it had been built was removed. A wooden strut (a "bostock") at either end stopped any movement until the moment of launch arrived. Retaining struts were knocked away and, picking up speed, the boat slid towards the water, pushing a surging wave across to the opposite bank as it made first acquaintance with its new environment. After further fitting out and painting the boat was ready for work.

But not all boatyards were small family businesses concerned only with the building and repair of narrow boats. *Pictured below* is a scene on the River Weaver at Northwich where W J Yarwood & Sons traded as shipbuilders for seventy years from 1896. They built a wide variety of boats - in iron and steel as well as wood - including tugs, one of which is seen in the background. In the foreground is the steel dumb barge "Parbold", being prepared for launching and work as a member of the fleet operated by the Lancashire millers H & R Ainscough. 72 ft (22 metres) long and able to carry 60 tons of grain these barges were towed across the Mersey to Birkenhead and up to Liverpool to pick up their loads, before journeying on to destinations on the wide Leeds and Liverpool Canal.

W.H. WALKER & BROS. LTD.
BOAT & BARGE BUILDERS

Yarwoods was one of the bigger and better known yards building boats for both independent bye - traders as well as for the larger canal companies. One of their larger orders - remarkable by narrow canal standards - was for 38 Town Class steel narrow boats for the Grand Union Canal Carrying Company completed between 1936 and 1937. Until the advent of cheap welding equipment after the Second World War few small yards could cope with the capital investment needed to begin building in steel. It was the larger yards with ship building connections like Yarwoods, and further south Harland and Wolff at Woolwich, who were best able to take on such work. A run of boats for the Grand Union was also undertaken there. Other significantly sized yards still continued to build in wood. One such was W H Walker Bros who established their business at Rickmansworth on the main Grand Union line in 1905. Pictured *opposite* is one of the twelve Star class motor boats that, along with paired butties, they built for the firm between 1935 and 1936. One wonders what boatmen must have made of such fanciful names as *Formalhaut*, *Grus* and *Merope*. However as Ricky built boats had a reputation for handling well they were probably fully content with their new craft.

Hauled up out of the water the underside features of this example of a Star class boat show up clearly. Horse drawn boats and butties came together in a sharply pointed stem from which hung the heavy wooden rudder with reversible tiller above. Their cabins were built low for no propeller shaft needed to pass below. In contrast the cabins of motors, such as this, were higher while their rounded sterns were built with a distinct counter to ensure that the propellers stayed well surrounded by water. Without this counter the water would be churned up to leave the propeller circulating in a foaming pocket of air, much to the detriment of propulsion. The countered stern helped avoid such "cavitation". Above the steel rudder is the typically Z shaped tiller of a motor, together with its detachable tiller bar. Two portholes let light into the boat, the rear to the cabin and the forward light to the engine room whose (engine hole) door stands open beyond. Carried on the wooden stands are the top planks that run the length of the hold. Forward is the covered triangular fronted shape of the cratch. Originally these storage areas were used as the fodder store on horse drawn boats.

A working boat can quickly deteriorate.The bumps and scrapes of locking, going aground and coming up hard against wharves combined with the impacts of loading and unloading all tend to damage and distort. Heat and cold alternately expand and contract structures, while water is always on hand to penetrate and rot. A narrow boat would usually be docked at two yearly intervals to be refurbished and repaired. Large companies had spare boats on hand to allow their crews to keep working. Smaller bye - traders and individual owners - the Number One's - would often hire a replacement boat from the yard doing the work on their own boat. Docking took place if possible in the summer as without ice in the wood it was easier to spot any rotting sections. Rarely would a boat enter a true dry dock. There were some; the Shropshire Union for example having a covered dock in the Chester basin, drained by emptying its water into the River Dee some way below. Most docking, however involved a slipway. The boat would be hauled out, inspected and repaired. Meanwhile the cabin would be fumigated with a sulphur candle and repainted throughout. After recaulking, external re-blacking and painting the boat would then be returned to work. Looked after in this way a narrow boat would last about thirty years. Even large boats were docked onto slipways. The Runcorn scene on the *left* shows a Mersey flat being recaulked, oakum being hammered in between her planks. Behind the railway bridge the Manchester Ship Canal is a reminder of an even larger inland waterway.

HORSE BOATING

On the waterways mechanical means to move the boats took a long time to become established. The power of the wind and, inland, that of animal muscles, remained significant well into the 20th century. We have grown familiar with towpaths alongside our rivers and canals, accepting them as normal everyday features of the navigations - but they were not always there. Upstream passage on a river initially involved gangs of men - the bow haulers - struggling to pull their boats through rapids, over shallows and against the current, while they themselves negotiated the hedges, marshy patches and fences along the way. Rough paths were worn by constant use but the millers and other landowners along the river banks did not always prove co-operative in providing the access needed. It was not until the 18th century when Acts of Parliament helped to formalise these navigations and gave their promoters legal powers to develop their waterways that much could be done to improve matters. Even then it took some considerable time - some important river navigations were still awaiting tow paths well into the 19th century.

From the outset canals were built with horse rather than human haulage in mind - an odd exception being the Stroudwater Navigation in Gloucestershire. Although opened to traffic in 1779 bow haulers stayed at work here for nearly fifty years more until, at last, a horse tow path was opened in 1827.

On the wider river navigations sail could be used - and indeed survived well into the 20th century, in some cases even into the 1950s. The sailing barges of the West Country and River Severn have already been encountered - while other important homes to sail were the Trent, Humber and Mersey estuaries, together with their river connections. Some sail powered craft from these waterways and others are *illustrated on page 79.* On the often square rigged and flat bottomed boats it was necessary to use lee boards when working these boats to windward - while on calm days or on narrower or shallow stretches shafting, bow hauling or more often horse haulage was needed.

But for over a century and a half the dominant, indeed essential source of power on the waterways was that of the horse. It is hard to overestimate the contribution that these animals made to the process of transporting goods by water, so allowing industrialisation to go on apace. And their work was to last for a very long time. Steam, and diesel power came late to the navigations, while some horse boats continued to work alongside their motorised successors until the end of narrow boat carrying. It was only in the 1920s that the balance really shifted towards motorisation - while throughout the 1950s horse drawn maintenance boats could be encountered on the Llangollen Canal and Clayton tar boats could be seen working in and around the Midlands. Indeed some horse drawn day boats still worked on the Birmingham Canal Navigations as late as 1970. It is interesting to note that even the rival railways recognised the utility of these animals, the last British Railways horses not being retired from shunting duties until 1967. Here they almost outlasted steam.

Pictured opposite is the harness used to attach a horse to its tow line, while below is shown the towing mast as mounted forward on the boat. Around the horse's neck was hung the collar into which the animal would lean when taking up the towing strain. High up on this are the rings that carried reins back from the bit and along to the driver who walked behind. Further rings carry them safely back. Attached to either side of the collar are the tug hooks. As the name suggests these, together with the back straps, transmitted the pulling strain along the traces on either side of the horse. The ropes are encased in hollow wooden bobbins to stop these traces rubbing and chafing the horse's flanks. At the back two ropes lead out to the spreader (sometimes called the swingletree) that takes the pull from the straps and towing traces. From this two short lengths of rope connect with a metal ring, and then the towing line itself. The long line of this cotton rope - usually between 80 ft and 100 ft in length (24- 30 metres) ran back across the tow path, over the water and up to the towing point. This wooden box mast was located a little behind the cratch, usually carrying the forward top planks as shown here. It was a hollow structure so as to allow an internal top mast to be raised or lowered within it. Depending upon the length of tow rope in use this telescopic arrangement allowed the rope to be kept out of the canal; a long line dragging in the water could create a lot of un - needed resistance. A locating pin ran through the topmast holes- at the head of which was the luby to which the towing line was attached. The tow rope could be quickly detached from the luby in an emergency; the possibilities of a bolting horse or an overrunning boat had to be catered for.

The bobbins along the traces were brightly painted, their mix of contrasting colours in similar vein to the cheerful cabin decoration of narrow boats. On southern Welsh canals and in parts of Yorkshire things were a bit more subdued, a leather tube rather than painted bobbins used to prevent chafing. The horses wore blinkers and above these in summer might be added a crocheted cap to keep the flies away. On high days and holidays polished horse brasses would complete the picture.

Horses themselves came in all shapes and sizes - although those under 15 hands height were preferred for work on those canals with low and restricted bridge holes. Almost all were mares or geldings. They came from a vast variety of sources and belonged to no particular strain or breed. In 1878 George Smith - the canal humanitarian whose work is described in a later chapter - wrote of the animals that "most of them were in the last stages of decay". This judgement is certainly not borne out by the photographic evidence of horses at work around the turn of the century. Most appeared to be well fed and in good condition; if not they certainly could not have coped with such long days of work as were required.

Ownership varied. The larger carrying companies such as Fellows Morton and Clayton had their own horses. The Shropshire Union owned over 300 at their peak and relied almost solely on horse traction until they sold out in 1921. The "number ones" - the small independent bye traders who owned both their boats and horses, sometimes used Shires to tow two boats at a time. On the broad canals it was a case of two horses being needed to tow a single flat.

Picture *above left* is a pair of "hanimals" at work on the Stroudwater. This term was used for the donkeys that, pulling side by side, hauled boats on many of the canals linking with the lower Severn. Donkeys were also used on a few other routes, as were mules; although smaller both were considered hardier than horses.

Pictured *below* is a "backering" scene. Trudging along the towpath together horse and driver would both work a very long day - sometimes up to fourteen hours on the move. The driver would walk along at the back of the horse, encouraging and steering if needed, but having to go ahead to set any locks on the way. The slow steady rhythm of horse hooves mixed with the creak of harness would continue almost unabated throughout the day, the animals growing so familiar with their task that on a particular canal they would come to know when to slow down for locks so as to allow the boat to glide gently into the waiting chamber. Experienced played a very large part in the efficient operation of a horse boat. Sometimes a whistle, a shout or a cracked whip might be needed to encourage the horse - while a clog, tied just behind the spreader so that it thumped along the tow path, might also be used to convince a flagging animal that someone was indeed close behind. On a family boat the children would take long turns at backering behind the horse.

The horse is feeding from a nose tin - for many a mile was covered while eating on the hoof. Early each morning and late at night, before and after the journey, the main feeds would be given - while two or three times during the day a nose tin would also be provided to allow the horse additional feed without any loss of travelling time. When the nose tin was removed it would often be replaced by a muzzle so as to prevent any pauses for grazing along the way.

A typical ration would comprise 70% or so of bulk foods, mainly hay but with the addition of straw and chaff. The remaining 30% was made up of oats, bran, peas and sometimes oil cake. Fellows Morton and Clayton, true to the high professional standards they set throughout their carrying years, issued a standard ration for their horses along these lines: to it would be added a small quantity of confetti to make their property easy to identify in cases of theft. In turn boatmen would add conditioning powders, vegetable scraps and other small treats. Drinking water for horses was usually taken straight from the waterway, the chill having first been taken off in frosty weather. On the Birmingham navigations, however, pollution was such that taps had to be provided along the towpaths - but the rural routes had very few of these.

The care of horses requires regular shoeing and veterinary support. The constant wear inflicted by hundreds of miles of towpath walking meant frequent visits to the blacksmith as seen at work *below*. Intervals between reshoeing were as short as two to three weeks. Larger companies provided stabling along their routes and blacksmiths were often located at these. The canal settlements as found around junctions would usually support a blacksmith, as would many boatyards. But in Victorian and Edwardian England few places were very far from a local smithy.

In addition to company stabling, independent contractors hired out accommodation to passing traffic. Making provision for horses was a widespread need in the days when these animals provided so much of everyday haulage and transport. Pubs would often have a loose box or two for hire in addition to providing refreshment and relaxation for the boat crews. Only rarely would recourse have to be made to a rug and tether along the canal bank.

The larger companies also provided veterinary care, but in practice traditional herbal remedies made from plants plucked from the hedgerows would often suffice. A common problem was that of collar sores; these could easily develop on the hard worked shoulders of the horse. Careful boatmen would ensure that collars were dry and warm before being placed over the neck - while a poultice based on oak bark and alum was used should sores still develop.

Towpaths were generally kept in good condition, wide enough to allow two horses to pass one another, and gently cambered away from the water to minimise the chances of falling in. Gravel surfaces were common, as were limestone chippings - particularly on the well maintained Shropshire Union system. Birmingham towpaths looked dull in comparison, built up from the ashes and slag left over from local industry. Canals towpaths provided an

unobstructed route, but on river navigations gates often had to be negotiated where the path crossed from one landowner's property to another.

The long towing lines used were easy enough to manage on straight sections but could cause problems on tight corners, at bridge holes and tunnels - and especially if the towpath crossed from one side of the water to the other. Pictured here is the elegant solution provided by the turnover (roving) bridges - this example being at Bank Newton just below the summit level of the Leeds and Liverpool Canal. Such bridges took the towpath back over itself to allow horse and boat to pass through the bridge hole without the need to release the tow.

Another solution was that of the split bridge. *Illustrated above* the driver is passing the towline through the narrow gap in the mid section of a cast iron bridge on the Stratford on Avon Canal.

Variations on this design were used on several other routes. Constantly in use these cotton lines had a hard life. The worn iron rubbing strips found at the corners of bridge holes remind us of the frictional wear that they had to contend with from the brickwork, coping stones and lock fittings of their working environment. Towline wear was always high and they had to be regularly replaced - usually at intervals of about five or six weeks.

Everyday life on a horse boat was a reflection of the particular working environment. In the Black Country of the midlands regular coal runs, from colliery to iron works and back again, week in week out, would make up the daily grind. In a rural area seasonality could provide for a bit more variety in route and cargo, but on the longer runs it was often very routine. In Cheshire, a county long renowned for dairy products, regular cheese fairs were held at Ellesmere and Whitchurch on the canal to Llangollen. Boats would load from here and from Nantwich every Saturday - to work through to Manchester for the Monday morning. One Shropshire Union boatman recalls that he "did nothing else for five years than to take cheese to Manchester".

Perishable goods like these needed a fast passage and boats would work "fly" to get them to their destinations as quickly as possible.

Scheduled fly boat routes were opened up to retain traffic in the face of railway competition. The "Shroppie Fly", still remembered in the pub of this name at Audlem, ran twice weekly loads of about 15 tons from Birmingham to Ellesmere Port in under 30 hours. Five changes of horse were needed on the way, with the "fly" taking precedence over all other traffic. On the Grand Union barrels of Guinness were hurried from the London brewery at Park Royal through to Birmingham - selected crews managing this journey in under 40 hours, rather than the more usual 4 or 5 days.

But whatever sort of schedule was being maintained all manner of boats, horse drawn or motorised, needed to reduce speed when entering a lock. The faster that these could be approached the less travelling time would be lost, so the technique known as "strapping" *as illustrated right* was devised to slow a brakeless boat as it entered a lock chamber. On the deck, below the tiller of the motor boat shown here, a length of rope with a spliced eye has been put over the "dolly". As the boat passed into the lock the helmsman jumped onto the walkway of the lock gate and, rope in hand, took a turn around the strapping post of the gate. As the boat enters the lock this now anchored length of rope will check the boat's speed and bring it to a halt. At the same time the gate will be pulled shut; efficient braking and economy of effort combined into one simple operation.

Although widely used not all canals provided strapping posts on their lock gates as did the Trent & Mersey shown *overleaf*. Other means of slowing down unpowered boats were therefore required. On the wide locks of the Grand Union the large bollards beside these could be used for strapping, particularly for the butty boats drifting in alongside to join their already stationary towing motors - but in such cases the gates still had to be shut by hand. If all else failed boats could be slid along the edge of the lock and the gate partly shut upon them, so pinching them to a halt; not a technique to endear itself to either the canal proprietors nor the boat owning companies. Many locks would have minor idiosyncrasies known to the boat crews who used them year after year. It was this build up of experience that made for efficient working - knowing exactly where shallows might slow down a boat, at what speed or angle each individual lock might best be approached, and how the wind would catch you when emerging from a particular bridge hole or onto a high and exposed embankment.

Once in the lock, with the water levels adjusted to allow onward progress into the next pound, came the job of getting the boat moving again. With steam or diesel this was straightforward enough, but with a laden horse boat a lot of effort was needed to make the standing start.

A useful technique to overcome the initial inertia of a stationary boat was that of "blocking". This relied on obtaining a mechanical advantage of 2:1 using a small pulley block. The picture opposite shows a horse boat being blocked out of a lock on the Worcester & Birmingham canal. A pulley block has been attached to the head of the towing mast. The tow line runs back from the horse, through this block and on to the small curved blocking hook seen on the side wall at the lock's tail. On the right - mid way between this hook and the mast - a toggle has been let into the line. As the horse moves forward the mechanical advantage provided by the block divides the haulage effort needed by half. The boat accordingly moves slowly but easily forward. The tow line continues running through the block until the toggle comes up against the pulley. The mechanical advantage is then lost, but the boat then moves more quickly. As it floats out of the lock the toggled end of the rope is pulled away from the blocking hook - and horse and boat move on to the next lock.

Blocking could also be used in locks with bollards rather than hooks-but this involved someone ashore releasing the tow rope - once it had gone slack as the toggle came against the pulley. Should a boat get stuck in a shallow bridge hole a stake knocked firmly into the bank could likewise provide the anchorage needed for blocking.

Waterways carried two way traffic - so provision had to be made to allow boats to pass one another without dispute, the tangling of tow lines or any other loss of time. Working procedures on the navigations were covered by bye-laws, determined and enforced by the controlling companies, and these normally specified the rules relating to rights of way. All gave precedence to fly boats, these being made easy to identify by a roundel or other device painted on their top planks or at some other prominent position on the fore end. Fines would be imposed on any boat crews failing to give way to this fast scheduled traffic - 20 shillings for a first offence and 40 shillings for each subsequent offence on the Grand Union in 1851. These figures are equivalent to £75 and £150 in today's money. Laden boats took precedence over the unladen ... and should two loaded craft meet then local conventions and bye-laws would come into play.

The driver of the boat giving way would pull away from the canal itself to stop his horse on the "hedge side" of the towpath. Meanwhile his steerer would guide their now slowing boat away from the path. No longer under tension its tow line would drop across the path and sink into the water.

The oncoming driver, meanwhile, moved towards the waterside of the tow path, he and his horse stepping over the now static tow line of the other boat. The horse and driver of the latter would then move on a short way, in order to keep up with their own slowly coasting boat, then pause a second time. The oncoming boat, without slackening speed, kept close to the bank to pass inside the stationary one, floating over its sunken tow rope in doing so. Horse and driver of the boat that had given way would then take up their own tow and continue on their way. "Passing lines" - *as pictured opposite* - was a matter of routine, smoothly taking place many times a day on the busier urban routes. On quieter country sections there would be a chance for a brief greeting and perhaps an exchange of news between the passing crews.

But not only horses had to use muscle power to move the boats. Shown below a Shropshire Union boat is being poled around to change direction at a winding hole. The child who waits patiently with the horse will spend her nights asleep in the tiny fore cabin, the top of which can be seen beneath the man's feet. On the shallow waters of the Norfolk broads sailing wherries would be quanted (poled) considerable distance on days when the wind failed.

Tunnels were expensive to build, so the extra width needed for a tow path was something of a luxury - even though in horse drawn days moving a boat through one was a far from easy task. If there was no towpath the horse would be led over the top of the tunnel to await the arrival of what had now become a man powered boat. A few tunnels were provided with chains to allow crews to haul along on them - while poling, although liable to damage walls and roof, was permitted in a few others. But "legging" was to prove the main method of moving boats underground for many years. Pictured *above* is a laden day boat being legged through one of the tunnels on the Birmingham system. Heavy hob nailed boots allow the leggers to get a grip on the slippery walls as they walk their boat along. In broad canal tunnels planks would be placed across the gunwales like wings and the leggers worked precariously from these. Progress was slow and a legged boat moved at no more than a quarter of a mile per hour.

Pubs at some tunnel entrances remind of the thirsty work involved, while close by other portals were the huts occupied by teams of professional leggers. Best known among these is probably Ben the Legger who made his living propelling boats along the 2048 yards (1873 metres) of the Braunston tunnel. It has been calculated that he legged well over 50,000 miles during his dank subterranean working life.

In broad tunnels the most common rule of the road was to keep to the right; one reason why stove chimneys, watercans and mops are normally found on the left hand side of narrow boat roofs. In narrow bore tunnels, where passing was not possible, debate over rights of way could flare into hostility. In May 1851 two boats met mid way along the twisty 1¼ mile length of the Oxenhall tunnel on the Hereford and Gloucester canal. Neither would give way. As well documented in the local press of the time they refused to move for 58 hours, while angry queues built up behind them. From mid-day on a Thursday until the following Sunday morning they obstinately sat it out. It is not recorded how the dispute was eventually resolved.

STEAM AND DIESEL

Much as the Duke of Bridgewater had shown the potential of artificial waterways by cutting his canal to Manchester, so it was a railway, running west from this self same city to Liverpool, that was to provide the crucial public demonstration of the potential of steam traction. At the Rainhill trials of 1829 the Stephensons' locomotive the "Rocket" clearly showed what this new form of mechanical power could achieve. But it was to take a hundred years or more before powered boats were to become the dominant force upon inland waterways- and by this time they were mainly being propelled by vaporised diesel oil, rather than by steam.

Many of the early experiments and successes with steam boating took place in Scotland, while as early as 1793 a steam powered paddle steamer had been tried on the Sankey Canal in Lancashire, shortly to be followed by similar experiments on the Bridgewater Canal. In a number of specific circumstances steam did manage to catch on as a source of power, to the extent that the Grand Junction Canal's carrying department came to use a number of steam tugs, one of which was to cause a disastrous explosion in 1874. A train of five barges was being hauled through north London on the Regents Canal. A spark from the chimney of the steam tug "Ready" landed upon the barge "Tilbury" - whose cargo included several barrels of petrol and five tons of gunpowder. A number of boatmen were killed in the ensuing blast which was heard loud above the hubbub of the city and up to ten miles away.

But it was not such inherent dangers nor lack of technical sophistication that weighed against a general transition from horse to steam power; it was more a matter of its particular characteristics not fitting in well with the the working conditions found on waterways. Steam is at its best when steady power outputs are needed - the haulage of a long goods train or the steady pumping of drainage pumps in a mine rather than the constant stop-start life of a boat passing down a heavily locked canal. It was easy enough for a boatman to leave his well schooled horse to look after itself while he operated lock paddles and gates, but for one man to have also to cope with the demands of a firebox, boiler pressure and water levels in gauge glasses at the same time was not really practicable. A horse was also quick to get to work in the mornings and needed relatively little attention at the end of the day - but to have to wait for an hour or more while getting up steam before starting out, and then having to clean out ashpan and firebox, perhaps while moored among other boats of an evening, presented practical challenges that were not readily overcome.

Although steam could propel trains at high speeds upon rails it could never do the same upon water. Few canals had really long pounds unobstructed by locks, while the problems of wash created by fast moving boats imposed a low limit upon permissible speeds. Also the sheer bulk of steam engines, together with boilers and fuel stores, critically restricted their use on narrow boats.

But it was a different matter when a steam boat was used as a tug and did not have to fit in any cargo - and particularly so when called to work in places where horses could not reach. Tunnel towing provided such circumstances and it was as the motive power for tunnel tugs that steam came into its own. After a number of early experiments it was in the middle of the 19th century that tunnel tugs came into regular service on a number of routes, so putting their teams of professional leggers out of business. Pictured *opposite* is the tunnel entrance at Preston Brook, the longest of the three tunnels found at the northern end of the Trent & Mersey. Tugs started work here in 1864 and continued to haul boats through the narrow bores until the early 1940s. A timetable operated from 6.00am until 8.00pm each day, shifts of tugman keeping the service running. On arrival at the tunnel boats would tie up along the tow path, the horses would be unhitched and then walked over the hill by their drivers. The boats meanwhile would be linked into a train, the tow being taken from the T studs at their bows. At the stern horse boats were fitted with tunnel hooks - just below the gunwales on either side, immediately aft of the cabin. The tow was taken back from these to the following boat; in this way the lines were kept clear of rudders and tillers. As illustrated a string of half a dozen horses is being taken ahead of an equal number of boats - but trains could be considerably longer than just six. On the long Braunston and Blisworth tunnels on the Grand Union as many as twenty boats would be pulled through at at time.

The tugs on the Trent and Mersey were unusual in that spring loaded guide wheels were fitted fore and aft that allowed them to follow naturally the direction of the tunnel walls. While this made life a little easier for the operating crew it did nothing to diminish the foul smoke laden atmosphere in which they had to work. Within a year of the introduction of the tugs four ventilation shafts had to be sunk to alleviate matters at Preston Brook, but it was to remain an inherent problem on most tunnels served by steam tugs.

About twenty five miles further south on the same route the long Harecastle tunnel (2926 yards, 2675 metres) burrows under the high land that separates Stoke on Trent and the Potteries from the Cheshire plain.

Here, in an effort to overcome the smoke problem, electric propulsion was tried with some success. At first batteries, carried in an attendant boat, supplied the power to the tug - but in latter years it picked up its power from an overhead cable in tram and trolley bus style. Eventually horse boating died away, but the tug worked on until 1954 when extractor fans came into use to vent diesel fumes and maintain a reasonable atmosphere in the tunnel.

But out of doors and before the days of clean air legislation steam boats could work free of constraint and did so most effectively on wide lock free waters - conditions more common on the river navigations and wide canals of northern England. These wider waterways allowed beamier boats to be built, which in turn meant that the bulky steam engines and boilers took up a lower proportion of the available hull space than on a narrower craft. The Leeds & Liverpool Canal, and especially so on its long lock free pound of nearly thirty miles running up to Apperley Bridge, provided just such an environment - as did the improved river navigations to the east of the Pennines. *Above left* is shown one of the Leeds & Liverpool steamers that carried coal themselves as well as being used as the tug for several unpowered horse boats of the same general design. Several dozen were built and so effectively did they perform on this cross country route that the last of them worked into the 1950s before being withdrawn.

Despite their inherent disadvantages one company made a notable commitment to steam driven narrow boats and used them very effectively in a specialist role for many years. Fellows Morton and Clayton, formed in 1889, was an amalgamation of several separate carrying companies. Central among these was the Fellows company, under the highly efficient direction of Joshua Fellows, son of the founder, and with an experience of steam boating going back at least fifteen years. Fellows had bought steam tugs from the Grand Junction when it gave up carrying shortly after the Regent's Park explosion. He obviously appreciated their abilities for between 1886 and 1927 thirty two steam driven narrow boats were to be built, mainly at the Fellows Morton and Clayton boatyard at Saltley, Birmingham and added to their extensive fleet of horse boats.

The picture below clearly shows how a boiler and engine unavoidably take up carrying space. The steamer "*President*" has about ten tons of potential pay load taken out of commission by the bulky and weighty machinery within the engine room. This limited her to about fifteen tons of cargo. In contrast the butty "*Kildare*" can take a load of at least twenty five tons. "*President*" and "*Kildare*" are both now preserved by the Black Country Museum.

To emphasise the power and speed that these boats could offer - was reflected in such evocative names as "*Admiral*" and "*General*", "*Monarch*" and "*Emperor*"- and to get the fullest possible value from their high initial building costs they had to be worked fast and long. Accordingly the steamers operated express "fly" services northwards up the Grand Union Canal from the City Road basin in London. At Braunston junction some of the fly services would go on to Birmingham while others branched off for Leicester, Derby and Nottingham. Their timetables were strict and demanding and it was said that a steamer and butty could always be found within a few minutes of their due time at any point *en route*. It made little sense to use such a high cost service to carry relatively low cost bulky materials such as coal and minerals. These were left to the cheaper horse boats also operated by the Company. Instead the goods carried were usually of comparatively high value:- barrels of turpentine and perishable foodstuffs, HP sauce and canned goods; sugar and tea, cardboard for the Players tobacco works in Nottingham and soaps and perfumes returning south from the Boots factory there. At the more important points along their routes the Company had a number of depots with warehousing. From these the horses vans and carts of local haulage firms would collect and distribute the goods delivered by water, but in the 1920s Fellows Morton and Clayton sought to build up a more integrated service and started to deliver themselves, building up a fleet of lorries in order to do so.

The steamer crews were hand picked and worked non stop, seven men on duty at a time; four men on the powered boat - always including an engineer on duty below - with three other crewmen aboard the butty. Smart uniforms of white overalls and cord trousers were worn by those working outside while the enginemen, down below in the heat and noise, wore the light blue overalls that became known as "slop". Although a hammock down in the engine room provided somewhere for a crew member to rest these were essentially working boats without proper living space, for the crews lived ashore. Only the steamer captains were directly employed by Fellows Morton and Clayton, being paid directly to take charge of the boat and its cargo. The remaining six crew members were then paid out of this lump sum by their employing captain.

However, despite the prestigious and reliable service that these coke fired boats provided and the number of faithful customers who remained with the Company over many years, the high labour costs involved in always having to have extra hands to work in the engine rooms were to prove insuperable. As the First World War approached Fellows Morton and Clayton started to cast around and consider alternatives to steam for their faster services.

A lead had been given by a very different sort of Company, one which used boats for its own purposes rather than providing a carrying service for others. The chocolate manufacturing firm of Cadburys had a number of waterside factories in the West Midlands and built up a small fleet of boats to serve these. Raw materials such as sugar and chocolate crumb were boated between the factories while a famous advertising poster of the 1930s showed a pair of their horse boats loaded with churns collecting fresh milk for their plant on the Shropshire Union. But their most significant contribution to waterways development had been made some time earlier. In the summer of 1911 they had introduced a steel narrow boat powered by an internal combustion engine, "*Bournville 1*"- shortly to be followed by her sister "*Bournville 2*". Horse feed, coal and coke were about to be joined by diesel fuel as a new source of energy upon the narrow canal network.

Within a year of the appearance of the Cadbury's motor boats Fellows Morton and Clayton were to take steps to follow this lead. In 1912 their new boat "*Linda*" was launched - powered by a 15hp single cylinder Bolinder oil engine. She was to be the first of many.

Bolinders were a Swedish firm whose main line of business was making engines for marine fishing vessels, but they also proved well suited to life on the English waterways. Slow revving semi-diesels, that needed a blow lamp to warm them up before being cranked into life, they proved themselves efficient and reliable. They took up half the space of a steam engine and allowed for an extra five tons of payload aboard. The slow task of bunkering with coke became a thing of the past as refuelling, illustrated in the Braunston scene on the *previous page*, was now a matter of one person with a fuel line. But the crucial advantage that was to make steam redundant was that the new engines did not require an extra crew member to man them. The distinctive boink-boink-boink sound of the Bolinders at work and the exhaust notes of various other makes of oil engine quickly replaced the hiss of steam. During the 1920s FMC converted the majority of their steamers to oil engine power, the last one working from London to Uxbridge in 1927.

Very rapidly a different approach to carrying on the narrow canals started to emerge as the new dispensation took effect. The "pair" was to become the working unit. Motor boats started to take over from horses as the dominant motive power, while ex horse boats became towed "butties" behind. The oil engines took up a 6 foot (1.8 metre) square covered space ahead of the living cabin, to which access could be gained by doors opening on to a narrow walkway along the gunwales. Through this the engine could be readily reached and fuel added to the the tanks below. Slow revving diesel type engines are very reliable as a rule, but *illustrated opposite* in a 1950s scene, a British Waterways mechanic has arrived in a service van to gain entry to the engine 'ole and make some emergency repairs.

On a pair of family working boats the cabin of the "butty" would usually be used as the main living space. Through the open cabin door the hard working woman could keep an eye on the food cooking on the stove and carry out other household tasks while simultaneously remaining on steering duty. *Illustrated above* a butty is being "rowed" around a tight turn by the steerer pumping away at the helm as she is towed along behind the motor ahead. When children were aboard as part of the family unit they would usually sleep on the motor boat.

It has been calculated that a pair of working narrow boats carried nearly a mile of rope between them. Much of this was used for the thinner "strings", the non load bearing ropes such as the "tying strings" that secured the cloths over the cargoes. The heavier load bearing ropes were generically known as "lines"- several of them having specific names. The thick towing lines of 70 feet (20 metres) or so that ran between a motor and butty were called "snubbers"; long lines being needed to keep the butties out of the wash of the motors, so making for a more comfortable ride as well as for easier steering.

Much shorter and more easily handled tow lines - "snatchers" - were used when working narrow boats side by side through the broad locks of the Grand Union. The motor would enter the lock to one side and release the tow so that the unpowered butty could glide in alongside. As the motor drew out again the short snatcher would be quickly re-attached and the tow taken up once more. Life was much harder when working a narrow canal with a pair of boats - as only one of the pair could fit into a lock chamber at a time. Normal practice was for the motor to pass through the lock and the butty then to be manually hauled into the chamber in her turn. Bow hauling, albeit in restricted form, thus lasted throughout the whole era of narrow boat carrying.

On long flights the alternate working of the motor through each lock, followed by bow hauling the butty through afterwards was a slow and exhausting task, but the less demanding technique of "lock lining" provided an alternative. On the Audlem flight of the Shropshire Union *pictured left* 15 locks occur in the space of one and a half miles. As these are nearly all evenly spaced it was an ideal site for lock lining. Four or five towing lines would be joined together so as to stretch between the two boats and along the length of the pound between the locks. There was now no need for bow hauling - just good team work and clear signals from one crew to the other. Motor and butty together would move into their respective locks, separated by the length of the extended tow line. Both locks would be filled and the top gates then opened. The motor would move forward to enter the next lock while the butty would simultaneously be hauled into the vacated lock ahead. Both uphill and downhill lock lining took place, although it was better suited to uphill work as shown here.

The ability to vary the length of a tow rope to suit a particular set of circumstances was not only of use when lock lining. "Running blocks", as shown on the top planks of the butty *below* provided another and more flexible approach.

On relatively straight stretches of waterway a long tow was to be preferred, but on narrow or winding stretches a shorter tow helped avoid the snubber becoming caught up on the banks and hedges at tight corners or at bridge holes located close to bends. Likewise when coming into the tighter confines of a canal basin or up to a wharf a short tow was also advantageous. To convert from a normal tow to long lining, or from a normal to a short tow length as when using a snatcher, required both boats to stop for a while - so some method that allowed the length of the tow line to be varied while on the move would obviously be of help. Running blocks allowed for this. On the butty as *pictured* on the *previous page* these horseshoe shaped blocks are located on the top planks behind the towing mast. The tow from the leading motor boat runs back to butty, through a pulley block on its towing mast, and then on through the running blocks to a stud on the cabin top. Here the tow was made fast and the steerer could let it out or take it in as circumstances required. It was not entirely without disadvantage, for taking the pull from from the motor back to a cabin top put heavy loads on it for which it was not really designed. These loadings could cause minor distortions and subsequently leaky roofs. The use of running blocks was rather patchy, more popular with some companies and on some routes than on others.

For profitable and economic operation a working boat needs to spend as much time as possible carrying a pay load, for empty running pays no bills. While "back cargoes" were eagerly sought they could not always be obtained - but at least running empty gave some respite for the crews. A pair of empty boats could be "cross strapped"- the butty pulled up tight against the stern fender of the motor by short lines from her forward T stud to the dollies on the rear deck of the motor. The two boats could then be moved along as a single unit, the straps between them forming an articulating joint between the two "halves". The butty needed little if any steering and on straight waterways the tiller could be held in place by tying strings across to the cabin sides, giving the steerer at least a partial break.

On broad canals two empty boats could be "breasted up" so as to be able to travel side by side, both along the pounds and into the locks themselves if sufficiently wide. This technique was essentially used for empty boats, for when they were laden single handed steering from the motor became very heavy and difficult. It was however sometimes used with laden boats on short streches between locks, or from a lock to an adjacent swing bridge. At the low speeds reached in such circumstances the handling difficulties were outweighed by the advantages of having a spare pair of hands ashore to work paddles, gates and winding gear.

The illustration *above* shows a scene at Marsworth on the Grand Union, two boats from the Grand Union Canal Carrying Company fleet "breasted up" together in a lock. They are tightly tied at stem and stern with the tiller on the butty, although out of sight, held in a straight ahead position with light rope "strings". This arrangement allowed the boats to be worked by just the motor's steerer.

On the balance beam of the gate sits the lock keeper, swinging his legs and taking a brief rest while still keeping an eye on the passing scene. Behind him is the lock keeper's cottage. On narrow canals boat crews normally worked the locks themselves, the keepers being responsible for general oversight and care, for minimising water loss and in the early days for opening up and closing down at dawn and dusk. On some of the northern broad canals and river navigations, and especially so on those with mechanically operated equipment, the keepers became operators as well as overseers, on some routes controlling access to the chambers by means of hand operated signals and even traffic lights.

On a quiet rural route the right of access to the locks would be taken for granted; they were there to be used, to be filled or emptied and the gates set ready. To ensure that a "good road" lay ahead that is that the locks were set ready for the oncoming boat - a member of the boat's crew would be sent ahead "lock wheeling" as seen *below*. On long pounds the bike was shipped aboard - but ahead of locks, swing bridges or any other features that needed prior attention to permit passage and minimise delay the lock wheeler would ride ahead to get things prepared.

On a busy and crowded route matters could become more fraught. A steerer would certainly not take kindly to find a lock being set against him for an as yet invisible boat - while disputes could also break out with both boats actually in sight, both steerers claiming their right of first passage through the lock. So on some routes a system of "first past the post" was put into place. Markers were set on the tow paths, equidistant from both sides of the lock. Whichever boat arrived at the post first could claim precedence - but human nature being as it is even this apparently equitable system could not totally eliminate friction or disagreement at locks.

A LIFE ON THE CUT

It is all too easy to take a romanticised view of the every day life of those who worked the canals in their heyday: bright colours on painted boats presenting a cheerful picture to the outside world, smoke drifting up from brass ringed stove pipes hinting at a cosy cabins within, mile after mile of sunlit dappled water gently sliding by - followed at dusk by the cheerful camaraderie of a canal side pub. Certainly holiday boating can recreate and emphasise such aspects of life aboard, which to a limited extent does reflect something of the reality. But on the other hand such views ignore the harsh unremitting existence of those members of an isolated and largely nomadic community - which from a combination of habit, ignorance and circumstance - continued to work for very low wages and under 19th century conditions until two thirds of the way through the 20th century - when finally this anachronistic and lingering way of life was to disappear.

In the earliest days of canal carrying much of the traffic was local and boatmen could return home at night. When the longer routes opened up several of the larger carrying companies organised shift working that allowed crews to remain almost entirely on their home stretches of water, exchanging boats with crews arriving from elswhere. In other cases hostels provided overnight accommodation for men obliged to travel further afield. At night locks would be chained off and traffic on the waterways came to a halt.

Railway competition brought in a new era. Boats on the waterways could only remain competitive if they were to be worked for far longer hours. Locks had to remain open to allow fly boats to work through the night, while the captains of the normal horse drawn craft, being paid by the load delivered, as well as having to work longer each day also had to cut down on labour costs. Women started to appear on the boats - unpaid, but taking a turn at the helm and at backering the horse as well as helping with the heavier tasks of loading and unloading; all in addition to their range of domestic duties. By the 1840s family boating on long distance cabin boats was being established on the narrow canals as a means to their survival.

Through the latter half of the 19th century the waterways struggled to compete with rail. Some river based navigations, notably the Aire & Calder and the Weaver did so with success. In contrast many canals were to fail in the last quarter of the century and to be abandoned. Most, but not all, of the late built waterways fell into this category. Alongside these the major long distance routes and the ever busy Birmingham canals settled down to provide useful economic services - and managed to survive.
They did so due to very low costs and minimal investment. The low costs were in no small part due to the working conditions of the boat people involved.

No doubt many of those who had been born into the home provided by a cramped narrow boat cabin and from which they emerged to work an eighty hour week, saw theirs as an inevitable and in many ways enviable way of life. After all it was shared by almost everyone they knew, and in their experience it had always been this way. Life "off the cut" was an alien world and many an old boatman has looked back with nostalgia to the freedom and self determination he believed the waterways provided. But legislation and unionisation were to nibble away at these certainties. In 1921 the Shropshire Union gave up carrying in the face of a potential eight hour day threatened by the unions of this railway owned canal. Two years later Fellows Morton and Clayton suffered a three month strike caused by their attempt to impose a 6.5% pay cut on their boatmen in order to stay competitive with the increasing threat of motor lorries. Although in response the Transport and General Workers Union proposed a 48 hour working week and did manage to get the pay cut slightly reduced the depressed financial climate of the time saw the boatmen going back to work for hours very little changed from those of eighty years before. British Waterways, following on the nationalisation that had taken place after the Second World War, certainly made attempts to enhance the lives of their boatmen, to provide better conditions on board and extra pay for extraneous duties. But in essentials the way of life found in the cabins of narrow boats across the system was to change remarkably little until it petered out with the end of carrying during the 1960s.

Pictured *opposite* is the interior of a typical horse boat cabin, looking out towards the stern. Here in a space 9 foot or so deep (3 metres) and little over 6 foot wide (2 metres), with just enough room for an adult to stand, the captain of a boat his wife and children would make their floating home.

Entry was via the rear hatches seen opening out onto the well deck beyond. The tiller is in its "out of use" position, curving up so as to take up minimum space. Beneath this and the T stud is the ventilated larder, and to the right the stove at which the woman stands cooking. Its chimney runs up and out to the top of the cabin and during a working day coal could be added from the store beneath the steerer's feet, so avoiding the necessity to leave the helm. Above the woman's head is the high mounted ticket drawer. Here paperwork relating to the boat, its cargo and passage past toll points would be kept. The bigger companies had arrangements for tolls to be paid on account but smaller traders and the boat owning Number Ones would normally pay cash. Food is served at a folding table that also acts as a door to the cupboard behind. Beneath it is a knife drawer and the pot cupboard used for crockery and cooking utensils. The man sits with his back to the bed hole pictured overleaf while to his left another woman and child sit upon the side bed. Beneath this is more storage space.

On a well kept boat the whole scene would be bright with light reflected from the polished brass of the oil lamp, hanging horse brasses and decorated ribbon plates. Lacework was hung up wherever possible and any uncovered surfaces were either painted with traditional roses and castles designs or wood grained paint. The stove, warm centre to the whole scene, was kept a shiny polished black and gave huge heat out into the tiny cabin. Looking back, as *pictured above*, is the bed hole. During the day bedding was rolled up into a cupboard, the door of which folded down to make a somewhat restricted double bed. To provide some privacy at night the curtains, seen drawn back here, could be pulled across -while to the right the side seat would come into use as a third bed. It was far from unknown for an additional child to have to sleep on a rug on the floor beneath. A few boats and particularly those built in the 20th century, had a small porthole in the side wall facing the stove, but the sliding hatch ahead of the tiller provided the main source of daylight and ventilation on most of them.

Until the coming of chemical toilets in the engine rooms of motor boats sanitation was at best a matter of a bucket, or more usually a nearby hedge or beneath a bridge hole in the towns. Quicklime would have to be put down in the most foul of these locations.

Women and children had a hard time of it, social opportunities and freedom of movement severely resticted by the mobile way of life. The youngest children had to be harnessed to the boat, while the older ones effectively became extra pairs of working hands.

It was a particular concern for the health and well being of the boat children that motivated the humanitarian reformer George Smith (1831-95) to lobby for improvements to their lot. There is no doubt that the life they experienced upon the waterways was rough and often brutal. The young were quickly put to work, backering a horse or taking the helm while learning of life from a world where fights over precedence at locks and drunken brawls at pubs took the place of any basic learning at school. Although the Education Act of 1871 attempted to make provision for efficient elementary education across the country it was never to achieve this aim upon the canals. Smith worked hard to draw attention to the squalor, vice and educational disadvantage that he saw, and at a time when the Victorians were experiencing a general awakening to the needs of "the lower orders" was instrumental in the passing of the Canal Boat Acts of 1877 and 1884. These introduced the inspection and registration of those boats also used as dwellings. The inspectors - as pictured below working in the final years of family boating - had rights of access in order to measure and inspect, so as to ensure that basic standards of space and hygiene were being met.

The Acts established that the cabins of living boats should provide a specified minimum of "free air space" for everyone aboard. 60 cubic feet (18 metres) was required for every adult, this reduced to 40 cubic feet (12 metres) for children under the age of twelve. Although far from generous these regulations provided for a real improvement in the living conditions of the floating population. Certainly it was a step forward from having to compete for sleeping space upon the floor or curled up on the cargo in the hold. The question must have crossed the minds of some inspectors as to how many children they were actually being allowed to see; no doubt many were hidden from view behind a hedge or on other boats when they came to call. But by the 1950s, as shown *overleaf*, the two children peeping out from beneath the cloths on "*Ayr*" would certainly have been accounted for. Segregation of the sexes was also required. The cabins slept in by husband and wife were registered for three adults only, so growing children (girls over twelve and boys over fourteen) soon needed relocation. As a result tiny fore cabins (*as illustrated on page 51*) started to be built into horse boats, while still later the coming of motors and working of pairs meant the availability of an extra full sized cabin.

Inspection was by Local Authority, eventually under the national oversight of a Chief Inspector to the Local Government Board, this tightening up implementation considerably. The place and number of registration had to be clearly shown,thus for example the FMC motor "*Hawk*" had *Registered at Uxbridge No 555* clearly painted on her upper cabin sides. A certificate giving the boat's details had to be carried aboard. The registering authorities were also required to ensure that the children received a proper education, but in practice this proved impossible to enforce. As an NSPCC report of 1910 observed "it is certain that the provisions of the Act ... for education ... are a dead failure". Illiteracy remained endemic among the boat people so that toll clerks became used to being asked to help with the reading of letters. Schools at Braunston and Ellesmere Port made a point of taking in canal children whenever they could, the Grand Union ran a floating school in an old barge at Bulls Bridge, and in the 1950s a small hostel was opened to allow residential schooling in Birmingham - but a few initiatives such as these could do little to cope with the educational needs of a self contained and isolated population, constantly on the move.

Even such everyday activities as shopping presented a challenge. Time spent stationary meant longer journey times, and money lost. Audlem, pictured *opposite*, provided a better chance for shopping than did most canal side villages. Here the long flight of locks gave the women at least some time to make their purchases while the boats climbed the 90 foot rise.

BRIDGE INN
78

This conveniently placed spot, mid way along the main line of the Shropshire Union, was to cater for passing boat people for over 120 years, from the canal's opening in 1835 until the final oil boats of theThomas Clayton fleet worked down the line from Ellesmere Port. Bonnets flapping and baskets over arms women would hurry up the slope from the tow path, past the Bridge Inn and along to their familiar shops; shortly to return with fresh bread, up to date gossip and the inevitable joint of meat. The basic diet for most boat people prior to the First World War was restricted by circumstance. Until this time the stoves on boats lacked ovens so that boiled meat was the norm. John Hollingshead, who in 1858 travelled up the Grand Junction canal on the boat "Stourport", wrote of the meal the all male crew sat down to one typical evening. "Large lumps of boiled beef mixed with slices of bacon were all fried together in a pan. When it was put upon a plate by the side of an eight pound mountain of bread ...it looked so fat, so very yellow and so very greasy..."

Potatoes were also a regular part of a diet that was more varied in the country than on the urban canals - for what could be poached from the woods or picked from the fields made for useful additions to the pot as well as for savings of cash. The crack of a gun bringing down a pheasant or pigeon would be disguised by a crack of a whip, while the dog that was carried on most boats acted as a retriever, carrying the unfortunate bird along to the next bridge hole for collection. Meanwhile the gun would disappear into the hold lest a gamekeeper came into sight. Diet was also supplemented by pilfering from cargoes. Sacks of flour and sugar would be split open for their contents while barrels of beer or rum would be tapped, topped up with water and then resealed; "Not short of quantity, only of quality" as the saying went. Each community generates its own code of conduct and definitions of morality. In the case of many boat people it was felt that the cargoes aboard their own boats were 'fair game", and the fields alongside the canals could rightly be treated their own linear vegetable gardens.

The woods and fields could also supply herbal remedies. Always on the move it was hard to find a doctor even if one was wanted, so these simple natural remedies, handed down the generations, usually sufficed. Hospitals were seen as places to be avoided and only sought out in the not infrequent cases of bad injuries sustained by accidents at locks, from kicks from horses and while loading and unloading. As a consequence of damp living conditions and the poor ventilation of cabins respiratory diseases were also rife.

Most boat people, no doubt through force of circumstance, preferred to be medically self sufficient. Up to as many as half their children came into the world in a boat cabin rather than on shore, the boats stopping only for a minimum of time. At Ellesmere Port a company nurse was employed , while at Stoke Bruerne the well known Sister Mary Ward provided invaluable assistance to many boating families into the final years of carrying. However such medical provision was very much the exception to the self sufficiency rule.

Until the middle of the twentieth century, when clothing started to become less obviously linked to the nature of employment, what one wore gave a fairly clear indication of how and where one fitted into society. Certainly this is true of the uniformed Pickford's boatmen of the 1820s who stands on the left of the back row in the picture *below*. Company identity and a pride in appearance was reflected in these optimistic early days. Pickfords were major canal carriers at this time, but in the difficult years of the mid 1840s switched to road transport and eventually evolved into the removals firm we know today. Next on the right stands a boatwoman of the mid 19th century; mob capped she wears a short knitted shawl over a printed bodice, little different from most of the country women of her time. Only as family boating developed did a more distinct women's costume start to emerge.

In the centre of the back row (*overleaf*) stand two uniformed employees of important canal companies; the proud moustachioed Captain of an FMC steamer from about 1904 and a pill box hatted worker from the Leeds and Liverpool. This was the time of high Edwardian "summer" when there was pride and panache aplenty. Not only steamer captains but many toll and lock keepers wore uniform. FMC provided their captains and mates with light cord trousers, wide leather belts from which windlass would often protrude, waistcoats with brass buttons, and flat caps to top it all off. To the right is a woman from the 1920s, children from about this period making up the front row of the miscellany. By this time the distinctive boatwoman's bonnet was well established, a curtain of lace hanging down over the shoulders and smart white blouse completing a proud and confident picture. After Queen Vicroria's death these bonnets were often black. Moving further right is seen a couple from the 1930s. Clothing is more subdued; the man in flat cap, jacket and waistcoat, the woman sheltering behind her shawl. By the 1950s (as seen to the extreme right) an anonymous boiler suit and peaked cap does little to distinguish this waterways employee from those in other trades. His wife would have dressed in as best she could afford, a little out of date perhaps - but in general keeping with the times.

Domestic life was never easy on the waterways. No doubt by the late 1950s the woman seen opposite hanging out her washing on "*Cylgate*", a boat from the Barlows of Birmingham fleet, would gladly have swopped on board boiling and scrubbing, followed by a mangle on the tow path for one of the new washing machines that were starting to appear in suburban homes. By this time family boating was in rapid retreat. After several generations afloat families were increasingly leaving the cut. Some went gladly, to an easier more comfortable life. Others went reluctantly and sadly, never content away from canals. The big freeze of 1963 and the demise of the British Waterways fleet heralded the end for most, but for nearly ten more years day boating on the Birmingham system just managed to survive. To avoid having to turn on these confined waters the double ended Joey boats could hang rudder and tiller from either end, the tow horse pulling them overland to change boats or direction - or when going home when work was over. The towing mast could also be moved and *below* it is being carried away, together with the fire bucket that has kept both these boatman warm - to the very end of their narrow boat carrying days.

RIBBLE
RIBBLE
BEDFORD
HONEYSTREET
STEVENS
SONS

A MISCELLANY OF BOATS

By way of a tail piece this miscellany of boats shows something of the wide variety of craft found on waterways other than the Midlands canal network. The pictures have been arranged on a broadly geographical basis.

Starting at the top left hand corner, i.e. in the north west, is "*Ribble*" - a Leeds & Liverpool motor from this broad waterway across the Pennines. To the right a string of compartment boats, carry coal on the Sheffield and South Yorkshire Navigation, clanking along behind their tug. Beneath, and to the right, is another Yorkshire boat, one of the "West Country" Calder and Hebble craft - so named as they came from the West Riding. These would often travel east across to Manchester using the Rochdale canal, there perhaps to encounter the likes of "*Bedford*" a typical flat as traded on that broad canal and as pictured upper centre. The square rigged sailing boat (below "*Bedford's*" stern) is a Humber keel; one of the wide family of historic craft built to this general design, that had traded on the north eastern rivers and estuaries long before the canal age had got fully underway.

The dark single sail of a Norfolk Wherry is seen (upper right) just above some more East Anglian craft - a short string of fenland lighters as worked on the maze of drainage channels and linking rivers of the area. Beneath these is a steam barge busy on the Ipswich and Stowmarket Navigation.

Across the bottom of the page are craft from the south and west. In the bottom right corner the Stevens barge shown was mainly used for carrying timber along the River Wey, and would also have travelled out onto the tidal Thames. "*Unity*" above, a Kennet and Avon barge, is built to a very similar general design.

The bottom row is completed by a Thames "western" barge of the type that traded on the upper tideway of this river, and to her left the other sailing barge is from further along the coast and the estuaries of the south west penninsula around the River Tamar.

Into the Bristol Channel drains the River Parrett. The boat with the long sweep over her bows is from the complex of Somerset waterways around here. Just above in the only Welsh boat in this miscellany, a horse drawn boat from the Glamorganshire canal, built to carry the iron and coal of this industrial area.

In sail to her right is a large Severn trow, bowling along with dinghy behind. Above, the tall funnel belongs to a Weaver packet, from whose decks Mersey sailing flats as seen upper left, would often have been sighted.

BIBLIOGRAPHY

It would be virtually impossible and not particularly helpful to produce a comprehensive bibliography for any book that ranges so widely across the waterways scene as does this.

Dr Mark Baldwin produced a useful general list in his *Canal Books*, published by M & M Baldwin at Cleobury Mortimer in 1984, while the bibliographies in the works listed below will allow particular themes to be investigated further. These books have been chosen for their relevance to the main sections of this work and between them could make the basis of a useful, albeit partial, waterways library. Unfortunately not all waterways books remain in print for long, so some of those listed here may be difficult to find.

Chaplin,T. (1989)
Narrow Boat
Whittet Books. London

de Salis,H.R. (1969)
Bradshaw's Canals and Navigable Rivers of England and Wales.
David and Charles. Newton Abbot.
(First edition1904: Henry Blackpole and Co, London)

Hadfield, C. (1950) as revised by Boughey, J (1998)
Hadfield's British Canals.
Alan Sutton, Gloucester.
(Originally published by Phoenix. Later updated and revised by David & Charles)

Hadfield, C (1968)
The Canal Age
David and Charles. Newton Abbot.
(Re-issued by Pan Books)

Hanson,H. (1984)
The Canal Boatmen 1760-1914.
Alan Sutton. Gloucester

Lansdell, A. (1994)
The Clothes of the Cut
Belmont Press, Harrow.
(Facsimile edition of the 1975 British Waterways publication)

Paget-Tomlinson, E.W. (1993)
The Illustrated History of Canal & River Navigations
Academic Press, Sheffield.
(Originally published as The Complete Book of Canal and River Navigations by Waine Research, Wolverhampton 1978, but now extended and revised)

Paget-Tomlinson,E.W. (1979)
Britain's Canal and River Craft
Moorland Publishing, Ashbourne.

Rolt, L.T.C. (1969)
Navigable Waterways
Longman, London.
(Since revised and updated by Bryan Marsh and republished by Penguin Books)

Ware, M.E. (1980)
Narrow Boats at Work
Moorland Publishing, Ashbourne.

Some useful **video material** is now becoming available and attention is drawn to the following for their excellent coverage of practical aspects of horse and motor boating. They can scarcely be recommended too highly.

Canals: Commercial carrying this century.
British Waterways Board. Distibuted by CFL Vision.

Towpath Encounter. Horse boating on the Worcester & Birmingham canal.
Sight Seen Partnerships. Distributed via the National Waterways Museum.

ACKNOWLEDGEMENTS

As with the Bibliography it is virtually impossible to acknowledge or indeed remember all those who have in some way or another contributed to this work. Its beginnings are to be found many years ago when, as a schoolboy, the author paddled a canoe along the then disused and almost forgotten lengths of the Kennet and Avon Canal and began to wonder what the waterways were all about. Since then the inputs have been many and varied: a wide range of reading, books, pamphlets and that indispensable magazine "*Waterways World*", miles spent walking the towpaths and yet more miles on the water itself, conversations with now retired and - alas - mainly departed boatman, and visits galore to the excellent museums with which this country is so well endowed. With some hesitation - for several important people may inadvertently have been missed - a list of those individuals who have particularly helped is shown below. Apologies to all those who may have been missed out.

But one person certainly cannot be forgotten; the illustrator of this book, Edward Paget-Tomlinson. His inputs have been so great that in a real sense this is as much his book as it is the author's, although the latter stands solely responsible for any errors or omissions that may have crept in. When drawing and painting Edward is able to inform his illustrations with that unique and extensive expertise which allowed him to so effectively write and illustrate his own award winning *Illustrated History of Canal and River Navigations*. This must surely be on everyone's shortlist as one of the most useful if not essential waterways publications yet to see print. I am most grateful to him for the patient and generous manner in which he has contributed to the development of this far less ambitious publication.

In alphabetical order other individuals who have helped include:-

Paul Bowen,
Mike Clarke,
Brian Collings, of the Waterways Museum at Stoke Bruerne,
Alan Faulkner,
Tony Hirst, formerly Director of the Boat Museum, Ellesmere Port,
David McDougall, Keeper of Collections at the National Waterways Museum, Gloucester,
Roy Jamieson, Archivist, British Waterways,
Richard Jones, former boatman,
Tony Lewerey,
John Stothert,
Peter van Zeller,
Les Wilson, former boatman.

INDEX

Indexing is by topic .
Illustrations are shown in italics.